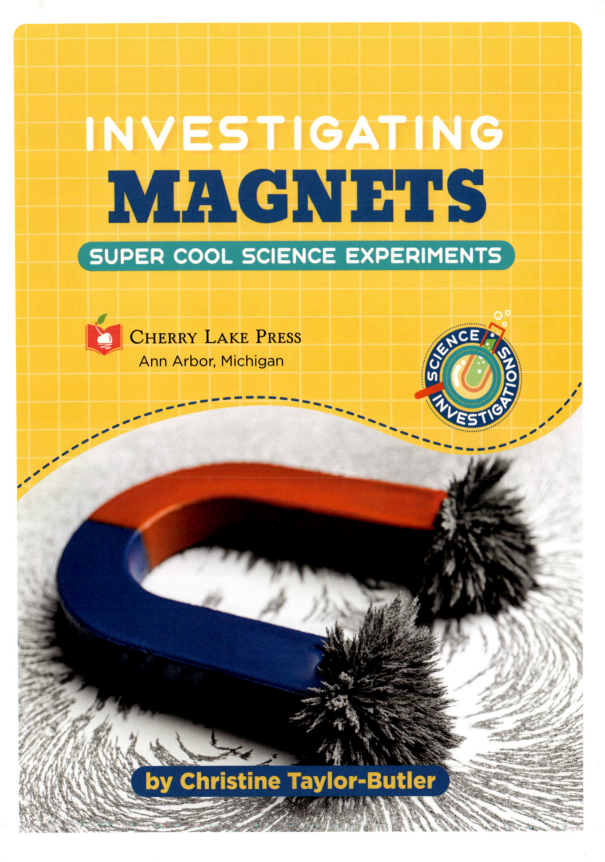

INVESTIGATING MAGNETS

SUPER COOL SCIENCE EXPERIMENTS

Cherry Lake Press
Ann Arbor, Michigan

by Christine Taylor-Butler

Published in the United States of America by
Cherry Lake Publishing Group
Ann Arbor, Michigan
www.cherrylakepublishing.com

Reading Adviser: Beth Walker Gambro, MS, Ed., Reading Consultant, Yorkville, IL

Content Editor: Robert Wolffe, EdD,
Professor of Teacher Education, Bradley University, Peoria, Illinois

Book Designer: Ed Morgan of Bowerbird Books

Photo Credits: cover, title page, © New Africa/Shutterstock; 4, 5, 9, 10, 13, 14, 17, 18, 21, 22, 25, 26, 29, 30, The Design Lab; 5, 6,7, freepik.com; 8, © Patty Chan/Shutterstock; 11, © Spiroview Inc/Shutterstock; 12, © ShutterStockStudio/Shutterstock; 16, © Pixel-Shot/Shutterstock; 20, © Pagina/Shutterstock; 24, © Andrey_Popov/Shutterstock; 28, © JpegPhotographer/Shutterstock

Copyright © 2026 by Cherry Lake Publishing

All rights reserved. No part of this book may be reproduced or utilized in any form or by any means without written permission from the publisher.

Cherry Lake Press is an imprint of Cherry Lake Publishing Group.

Library of Congress Cataloging-in-Publication Data has been filed and is available at catalog.loc.gov

Printed in the United States of America

A Note to Parents and Teachers: Please review the instructions for these experiments before your children do them. Be sure to help them with any experiments you do not think they can safely conduct on their own.

A Note to Kids: Be sure to ask an adult for help with these experiments when you need it. Always put your safety first!

Note from Publisher: Websites change regularly, and their future contents are outside of our control. Supervise children when conducting any recommended online searches for extended learning opportunities.

CONTENTS

Magic Magnets? **4**

Getting Started **5**

Experiment 1: **8**
Let the Force Be with You!

Experiment 2: **12**
Do Opposites Really Attract?

Experiment 3: **16**
Share the Power

Experiment 4: **20**
Which Way Is North?

Experiment 5: **24**
The Body Electric

Experiment 6: **28**
Do It Yourself!

Glossary 30
For More Information 31
Index 32
About the Author 32

Magic MAGNETS?

Take a look at your refrigerator door. Do you see any magnets? Maybe they are holding up your family's grocery list. How are magnets able to stay in place without falling to the floor? Is it magic? Nope. But what you are witnessing is still amazing. It's an incredible **force** of nature called magnetism.

Have you ever wondered how magnets work? If so, you are already one step closer to looking at the world around you through the eyes of a scientist. Can you believe that you can do **experiments** with things you already have at home? In this book, we'll learn how scientists think. We'll do that by experimenting with magnets.

Getting STARTED

Scientists learn by studying something very carefully. For example, scientists who study magnets look for places where magnets are found on Earth. They see which objects stick to magnets and which ones do not. They notice that magnets can sometimes make common objects magnetic. They do experiments to see how magnets can be used to power machines or to help us navigate Earth.

Good scientists take notes on everything they discover. They write down their **observations**. Sometimes those observations lead scientists to ask new questions. With new questions in mind, they design experiments to find the answers. You can design experiments and find answers at home!

When scientists design experiments, they often use the scientific method. What is the scientific method? It's a step-by-step process to answer specific questions. The steps don't always follow the same pattern. However, the scientific method often works like this:

STEP ONE: A scientist gathers the facts and makes observations about one particular thing.

STEP TWO: The scientist comes up with a question that is not answered by observations and facts.

STEP THREE: The scientist creates a **hypothesis**. This is a statement about what the scientist thinks might be the answer to the question.

STEP FOUR: The scientist tests the hypothesis by designing an experiment to see whether the hypothesis is correct. Then the scientist carries out the experiment and writes down what happens.

STEP FIVE: The scientist draws a **conclusion** based on the result of the experiment. The conclusion might be that the hypothesis is correct. Sometimes, though, the hypothesis is not correct. In that case, the scientist might develop a new hypothesis and another experiment.

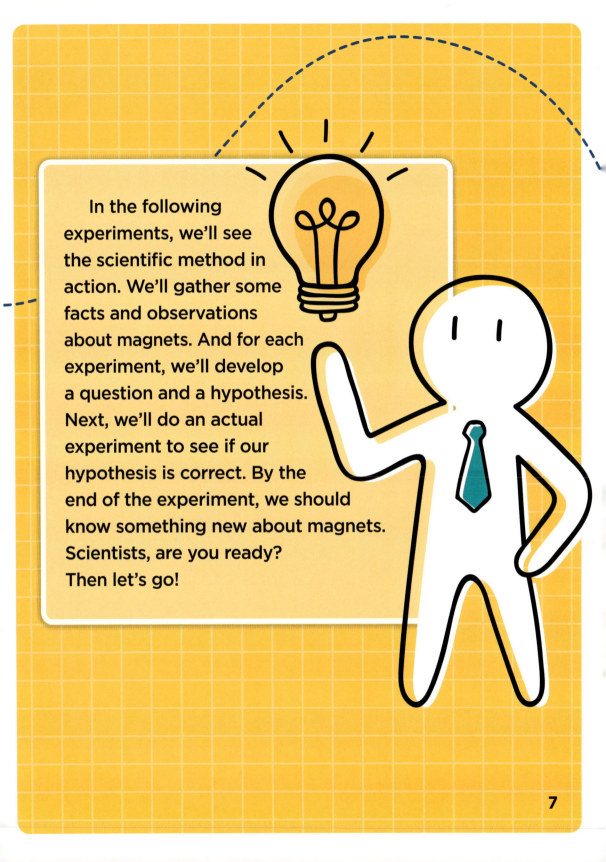

In the following experiments, we'll see the scientific method in action. We'll gather some facts and observations about magnets. And for each experiment, we'll develop a question and a hypothesis. Next, we'll do an actual experiment to see if our hypothesis is correct. By the end of the experiment, we should know something new about magnets. Scientists, are you ready? Then let's go!

EXPERIMENT 1

Let the Force Be with You!

First, let's gather some observations. What do you already know about magnets? You probably know that magnets have an invisible force that makes things stick to them. This means that magnets attract objects. For example, you may use magnets to stick papers to your refrigerator. In this case, the magnets are attracted to the refrigerator. These observations lead us to a question: Do magnets attract all things or just some things? Our hypothesis for this first experiment is this: **Magnets only attract things that are made of metal.**

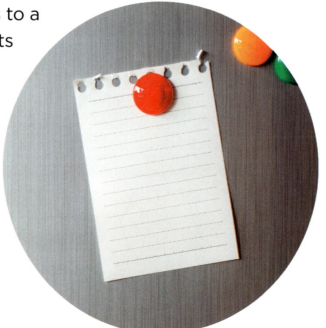

8

Here's what you'll need:

- A sheet of paper and a pencil to record your observations
- A horseshoe magnet or bar magnet
- A penny
- An iron nail
- A paper clip
- A steel ball bearing
- A dollar bill
- A small square of aluminum foil

INSTRUCTIONS

1. Which objects do you think the magnet will attract? Draw a line down the middle of your paper. Write "Attracts" at the top of the left column. Write "Does Not Attract" at the top of the right column.

2. Place the magnet on top of the penny and lift up. Does the penny stick to the magnet? If so, write "penny" in the left column. If not, write "penny" in the right column.

3. Repeat these steps with the nail, paper clip, and ball bearing.

4. Now fold the dollar bill in half. Hold the bill up by pinching the top edge of one of the folded halves. Let the other side hang down. Place the magnet close to the lower part. What happens? Try it with the aluminum foil. Do you get the same result?

CONCLUSION

After you've finished experimenting, look at your two-column chart. Which objects were attracted to the magnet? Do they have something in common? What do you notice about the items that were not attracted to the magnet? What can you conclude from this experiment? Does a magnet attract all types of metal?

FACTS!

Why didn't the magnet pick up the penny? It's made of metal, right? Magnets are only attracted to certain metals, including iron, steel, and nickel. Old pennies are made of copper. New pennies are made of copper and zinc. Those metals are not attracted to a magnet. There is one exception. In 1943, the government needed copper to use in the war. That year, pennies were made from steel instead of copper.

Did it surprise you that the magnet made the dollar move? Magnets are not attracted to paper. So why does the dollar have magnetic properties? Dollar bills are printed with ink that has iron in it. The magnet attracts the iron particles in the ink.

EXPERIMENT 2

Do Opposites Really Attract?

In Experiment #1, we learned that magnets are only attracted to certain kinds of metals. A scientist might wonder if magnets can do other things. Perhaps the scientist might ask this question: If magnets can attract certain types of objects, can magnets also repel objects?

Repel means to push them away. You may have noticed that a bar magnet has two letters on it: N and S. These are called the north and south **poles** of the magnet. So here's a new hypothesis to test: **Magnets always attract other magnets**.

Here's what you'll need:

- 2 bar magnets with ends marked "S" and "N"
- 2 refrigerator magnets
- A sheet of paper and a pencil

INSTRUCTIONS

1. Place the magnets far apart on the table. Take one bar magnet and place the end labeled "S" on a refrigerator magnet. Do the two magnets stick together? Now place the end labeled "N" on the refrigerator magnet. What happens? Write down your observations.

2. Put the bar magnets to the side. Place the two refrigerator magnets next to each other. Do they stick together? What if you turn one magnet upside down? What happens if you place the front of one magnet against the back of the other?

3. Now put the bar magnets on the table in front of you. Place the end of the first magnet marked "S" next to the end of the second magnet marked "N." Did they attract or repel?

4. Turn one bar magnet around so that the "N" side is facing the "N" side of the other bar magnet. Try pushing them together. What happens? Can you try to put the two sides marked "S" together?

5. Now try putting opposite sides together. Do you get the same results?

CONCLUSION

When scientists make a hypothesis, they are using what they know to make a prediction, or an educated guess. But sometimes the answer isn't what they expected. Did you get the results you expected? If not, that's okay. It's how discoveries are made. In this case, when magnets with opposite poles are placed together, they attract. When magnets with the same poles are placed together, they push away. Why don't refrigerator magnets work the same way? These flat magnets are created using a special process. The surface is made of magnetic materials arranged in a row: NSNSNS. Any type of magnet will stick to it, and it can stick to itself.

FACTS!

In China, Japan, and South Korea, scientists have used their knowledge of how magnets attract and repel to build high-speed trains. These trains do not have engines. Instead, the trains float above a magnetic track. Electricity is used to change the track's magnetic energy to push or pull the train. These trains can travel as fast as 286 miles (460 kilometers) per hour!

EXPERIMENT 3

Share the Power

In our last experiment, we learned that magnets are powerful. But a **magnetic field** is invisible. So it is not easy to see how much power a magnet contains. A scientist might wonder how far a magnetic field stretches. Can a magnet pick up more than one item at a time? Can it attract objects from far away? Here are two hypotheses you can test:

Hypothesis #1: Magnets can pick up more than one object at a time.

Hypothesis #2: Magnets can pick up items without touching them.

Here's what you'll need:

- A pencil and paper to record your observations
- A bar or horseshoe magnet
- 10 paper clips
- 10 safety pins
- 10 screw bolts
- A ruler

INSTRUCTIONS

1. Put each set of objects in separate piles. Move the magnet over the pile of paper clips. How many paper clips were you able to pick up?

2. What do you think would happen if you added more paper clips to the pile? Try it!

3. Remove the paper clips and wave the magnet over the pile of safety pins. What happens?

4. Try the bolts. Can you pick them all up? Try. What happens? Why do you think that happened?

5. Let's test the second hypothesis. Put your objects back into separate piles. Stand a ruler up next to the paper clips.

6. Put the magnet 3 inches (7.6 centimeters) above each pile. Can you attract anything from this distance?

7. Put the magnet 2 inches (5 cm) above each pile. What happens?

8. Try putting the magnet 1 inch (2.5 cm) above each pile. Is there a difference between lighter and heavier objects?

9. Next, place your paper clips in a single row. Use the magnet to pick up the end of the first paper clip. Now place the free end of the paper clip next to the second paper clip. Does the first paper clip stick to the second clip to form a chain?

10. Repeat step 9 with the pins and again with the bolts. Does weight or size make a difference?

11. Finally, try to make a chain of different items: one bolt, one safety pin, and one paper clip. What happens? Write down all of your observations.

CONCLUSION

You've seen that a magnet can pick up more than one item even if the magnet isn't touching it. But how? Metal, along with everything else, is made up of tiny parts called atoms. The ends of each atom have an electrical charge. When a magnet attracts an object, the atoms of that object line up so the electrical charge faces the same direction. For a few seconds, that object becomes a magnet. It is not very strong, but it can use its power to pick up another object. The second object has even less power. This keeps going until there isn't enough energy left to pick up another item. If you use a more powerful magnet, you can pick up more items before you run out of "power."

EXPERIMENT 4

Which Way Is North?

A **compass** is a useful tool. It can help keep you from getting lost when you are hiking. Let's start with what you know about a compass. A compass has a single hand that spins like a clock. But unlike a clock, this hand or needle stops spinning when it points north.

How does a compass work? From Experiment #1, we know that magnets are attracted to some objects. And we know from Experiment #3 that a magnet can turn an ordinary object into a magnet as long as that object is touching a magnet. But how does a compass know where to point? Let's experiment to find out. Here's a new hypothesis: **Earth has magnetic properties.**

20

Here's what you'll need:

- 2 large sewing needles
- 2 clear water glasses that are the same size (Make sure the sewing needles can fit sideways inside the glasses without touching the sides.)
- A ruler
- 8 inches (20.3 cm) of string
- A pencil
- A bar magnet
- Water
- A small cork

INSTRUCTIONS

1. Measure the height of 1 glass with a ruler. Divide that number by 2. Record that number.

2. Tie one end of your string around the middle of 1 needle. Now attach the other end of the string around the middle of the pencil. Make sure the length of the string between the needle and the pencil is equal or nearly equal to the number you recorded in Step 1.

3. Rub one end of the bar magnet over the long side of the needle. Always rub it in the same direction from left to right. Repeat 30 times. Don't poke yourself!

4. When you are finished, place the needle inside the glass, resting the pencil on top of the glass. What happens when the needle stops spinning? What direction is it pointing? Record your observations.

5. Fill the second glass with water. Place the cork in the water.

6. Rub the magnet over the long side of the second needle. Then set the needle on top of the cork. Does the second needle point in the same direction as the first? Record your observations.

7. Let the experiment rest for an hour. Are the needles still pointing in the same direction? Record your observations.

8. Recheck the experiment in the morning. Do you get the same results?

CONCLUSION

Why do you think the needles pointed in the direction they did? Which way do you think is north? Do you think that Earth has magnetic properties?

You may want to try some variations of your experiment. Try rubbing the needle 50 times or 100 times. Does the magnetic charge last longer? Can you think of other variations to explore?

FACTS!

Imagine if a giant stick ran through the center of Earth. One end would come out at the North Pole. The other end would come out at the South Pole. This is called an **axis**. Earth spins around it. The center of Earth is solid iron. It is covered with a layer of melted liquid iron. We know that magnets are attracted to iron. When Earth spins, the liquid moves. This creates a magnetic field. However, many people don't know that the planet's magnetic fields are flipped. The North Pole is actually charged like the south side of your magnet. The South Pole is charged like the north side of your magnet.

· EXPERIMENT 5 ·
The Body Electric

We know that Earth acts like a giant magnet. Some metals have a magnetic charge. Even the ink used to print our money has magnetic properties. But what about you? Does your body have magnetic properties as well? If it did, wouldn't your magnets stick to your hands when you performed these experiments? Let's try a hypothesis: **The human body contains substances with magnetic properties.**

Here's what you'll need:

- 1/4 cup of an iron-fortified cereal, such as Total
- A bowl
- A spoon
- The strongest magnet you can find
- 4 resealable plastic bags
- A hammer
- A cup of warm water
- A magnifying glass
- An iron-fortified adult vitamin

INSTRUCTIONS

1. Put 1 tablespoon of the cereal in a bowl. Mash it with the spoon until it is broken into tiny pieces. Place the magnet close to the cereal. What happens? Record your observations.

2. Now seal the remaining cereal in a plastic bag. Gently crush the cereal into tiny pieces with your hands. Lay the bag on a table or counter, and tap it gently with a hammer, breaking the cereal into a powder.

3. Pour the powder into a different plastic bag. Add 3 tablespoons of warm water. Mix well until it is a soupy mixture. Seal the bag.

4. Slide the magnet along the bottom of the bag. What do you see? Try looking through a magnifying glass as you slowly move the magnet. Write down your observations.

5. Slowly drag the magnet all over the bag of soupy cereal. Lift the magnet about 1/8 inch (0.32 cm) above the bag and move it from side to side about 1/2 (1.27 cm) inch.

Do tiny black particles of iron collect near your magnet? Move the magnet to a clean section of the bag. Can you see the iron now?

6. Repeat this experiment using a crushed vitamin and 1 tablespoon of warm water. Use the magnifying glass to get a close-up view.

CONCLUSION

Think about what you observed. Which has more iron: the cereal or the vitamin? What happens to the iron when you eat the cereal or vitamin? Does your body have magnetic properties?

FACTS!

The human body needs iron to keep its red blood cells healthy. Iron helps the blood carry oxygen. But how do you get iron into your body? Tiny amounts of iron are found in many foods you eat. Some companies add iron to foods such as cereals. Look at the nutrition facts listed on the cereal box. Are you surprised at how little iron there is? You don't need very much.

EXPERIMENT 6

Do It Yourself!

How about running a classic experiment on your own? Try to discover which part of a bar magnet has the strongest magnetic force. Where do you think the force might be the strongest? At the poles? Along the sides? Near the center? Come up with a hypothesis.

For your experiment, you'll need a bar magnet, a sheet of paper, and iron filings. You can find iron filings at a school supply store or a science supply store. Your teacher may also have some you can use. Place the bar magnet on a table. Lay the paper over the bar magnet. Sprinkle the iron filings on the paper over the area with the magnet.

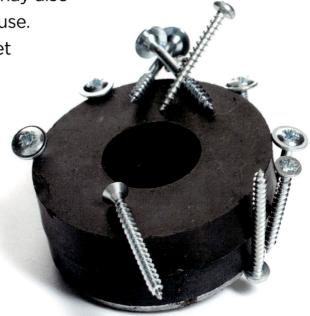

Slightly move the paper back and forth over the magnet. How do the iron filings react? Do you see any shapes or patterns? Do more iron filings move toward certain areas? What does this tell you about the strength of the magnetic field in these areas?

FACTS!

Okay, scientists! Now you know many new things about magnets. You learned through your observations and experiments. You even discovered that tiny magnetic particles are inside of you! So what's next? That's up to you!

Glossary

axis (AK-suhs) a real or imaginary line that runs through the center of an object, and around which the object turns

compass (KUHM-puhs) a tool that shows the direction of Earth's magnetic field

conclusion (kuhn-KLOO-zhuhn) a final decision, thought, or opinion

experiments (ik-SPEHR-uh-muhnts) scientific processes used to discover information

force (FORS) an invisible energy that can cause something to move

hypothesis (hahy-POTH-uh-sis) a logical guess about what will happen in an experiment

magnetic field (mag-NEH-tic FEELD) an area around a magnet in which the magnet has the power to attract or repel

observations (ob-zur-VAY-shuhnz) things that are seen or noticed with one's senses

poles (POHLZ) the ends of a magnet or a planet's axis

For More Information

BOOKS
Adler, David A. Anna Raff (illustrator). *Magnets Push, Magnets Pull.* New York, NY: Holiday House, 2018.

Crane, Cody. *Electricity and Magnetism (A True Book: Physical Science).* Danbury, CT: Children's Press, 2019.

Midthun, Joseph. Samuel Hiti (illustrator). *Magnetism.* Building Blocks of Physical Science. Chicago: World Book, Ann Arbor, MI: Cherry Lake Publishing, 2022.

WEBSITES
Explore these online sources with an adult:

A Kid-friendly Introduction to Magnets and Magnetism | HowStuffWorks

Magnets: An Invisible Force video | Science Trek | PBS

TIME for Kids | What Are Magnets?

Index

atoms, 19
attraction, 8, 10–16, 18, 20, 23
   experiments, 6–29
axis, 23

compass experiment, 20–23
conclusions, 7, 11, 15, 19, 23, 27

do-it-yourself experiment, 28–29

hypotheses, 6–8, 13, 15–16, 18, 20, 24, 28

iron, 9, 11, 23, 27–29

magnetic fields, 16, 23, 29
magnetic properties, 11, 20, 23–24, 27
magnetic properties experiments, 20–27
magnetism, 4
metals, 8, 11–12, 19, 24
metals experiment, 8–11

North Pole, 23
notes, 5

observations, 5–9, 14, 17, 19, 22–23, 26, 29

poles, 13, 15, 28

red blood cells, 27
repulsion experiment, 12–15

scientific method, 6–7
scientists, 4–7, 12, 15–16, 29
South Pole, 13, 23

trains, 15

underwater ecosystems, 28

yeast, 12, 14–15

About the Author

Christine Taylor-Butler is an author with degrees in both civil engineering and art and design from the Massachusetts Institute of Technology (MIT). When she is not writing, she is reading, drawing, or looking for unusual new science ideas to write about. She is the author of more than 90 fiction and nonfiction books for children.